The Art of
MANAGING UP FOR
CAREER PROGRESSION

SOLA OSINOIKI

TABLE OF CONTENTS

Acknowledgments

FIRST OF ALL, I would love to thank my wife Morounkunbi Osinoiki for all her support and encouragement on this journey. Even though she runs her own business that impacts kids, she still finds time to support all that I do.

Thanks to my four kids, Olu, Funso, Ola and Lola, who have had to share me with multiple companies, mentees and coachees that I have worked with. Yet they remain my strongest cheerleaders.

To Barry Ross, a mentor chosen for me by people wiser than me, and they were right. Barry helped me navigate my way through a key promotion in my life, exiting consulting, settling into industry again and combating any imposter syndrome I might have had on the way to where I am now.

To Paula Grohmann, a mentee at a time, who sat across my dining table and said, "You need to share your skills and knowledge with the world." Her suggestion led to the birthing of Josh Leadership Academy and the seeds for this book.

To Dr Kike Oduba, another mentee who worked with me to make this book a reality, editing, questioning and validating the content and who also kindly wrote the foreword.

To every manager I have ever had, to every leader whose organisation I have worked in, to every employer who gave me the chance to work in their companies and for all the mentors and coaches I had along the way.

To everyone I have worked with, you helped me accomplish all that I did. I hope that I made it easy for you to progress in your careers too!

Finally, I want to thank God for life, for every door opened and for every door closed. I am who I am because of Your grace.

Sola Osinoiki

Foreword

NAVIGATING THE NUANCES and challenges that come with making career changes in a fast paced world economy is usually not an acquired skill, it is an art. In his remarkable journey from a security guard, to holding a prestigious role as the Vice President of Global People Technology in a multinational company, Olusola Osinoiki has proven to be an exceptional model of managing up in healthy and unhealthy work environments.

If you are looking to advance your career to an executive role, change jobs or pivot into new adventures as a professional, this book will show you through the eyes of Olusola's experiences, ingenious ways to handle work relationships, unfavorable workplace conditions, uncharted work assignments and unpredictable changes in your career.

Invariably, the Art of Managing Up for Career progression will show you how to find the best opportunities in your work environment, how to be creative and carve out new opportunities for your career growth, and ultimately, how to take the best advantage of the opportunities you have.

In the words of a wise man I greatly admire, 'Many have been dealt a mixture of good and not so good cards in life, all of which contain the potential for big wins; only a few will win, if they know how to play their cards right'.

I encourage you to read this book with a winner's mindset and be prepared for some big wins in your future as you manage up for your career progression.

See you at the top!

Kike Oduba.
CEO Wellness Wits

Introduction

I AM NOT OBLIVIOUS to the fact that there are quite a number of books that have been written on "the Art of Managing Up." Some of these books do not only contain valuable information on the subject, they also treat the subject extensively. However, two things considerably set this present intervention apart from others.

First, this book is about the art of managing up, specifically in relation to career progression. I am particularly interested in providing some guidance to people who are interested in their career progression or those who are interested in helping their subordinates or mentees progress in their careers.

Second, this book stems from my years of experience in management. With a career spanning over three decades – from my very first job in Nigeria in the National Youth Service Corps (NYSC) to my current executive role, I have gained considerable experience and knowledge that I believe can help the next generation of people who need to manage up for career progression.

At some point in my career, it became clear to me that I had to manage my managers even though I was unsure of how to succinctly describe my experiences nor did I fully appreciate the dynamics involved. Nonetheless, I was determined to keep progressing and navigating the world of work to find a path through.

Some of my actions were done instinctively, some by trial and error, and others I was constrained to learn by reason of what life threw at me. It has been a blast and profoundly rewarding journey. I am excited to be sharing my story with you in this book.

I have come to realise that there are two sides to the coin of managing up. One is managing up in a healthy environment, that is, managing up with a boss with whom you have a good relationship. The other is managing up in an unhealthy environment; that is, managing up with a boss with whom you do not have a good relationship. I could have used the word "toxic" as it is commonly used in contemporary times; but I prefer to use the words "healthy" and "unhealthy."

Having experienced both environments and successfully progressed in my career through managing up, I hope the insights I share in this book inspire you on your journey of career progression as well. So come on the journey with me!

1

My Story

MY STORY STARTS in Lewisham, a little town in London, United Kingdom from where I have so many fond childhood memories. At the age of eight, my parents moved to Nigeria, where I finished primary and secondary school. Thereafter, I went to study Civil Engineering at one of Nigeria's foremost federal institutions of higher learning, Obafemi Awolowo University. Upon graduation, I was mobilized for the mandatory National Youth Service Corps (NYSC) program. NYSC is akin to national service in other countries, where graduates serve their nation for one year. The aim of the NYSC service year in Nigeria is to foster unity in a nation that has over 200 languages. I was assigned to the Eastern part of Nigeria, which meant relocating from Lagos where I was living with my parents. Over the next 12 months, I worked as an Engineer, building roads and bridges in a town called Agbor in Delta State.

After completing my youth service, I was unable to find employment as an engineer. I did not want to sit at home idle and unproductive, and so I began to think of what else I could to do in the interim. As it happens, I had always had a passion for publishing, and had once considered a career in the industry. It was therefore an easy decision to accept the role of an editor with a Christian publishing firm when the opportunity opened up for me.

Soon after, my fiancee (now my wife) left Nigeria for the United Kingdom (UK) to complete her first degree. There had been a number of student protests in Nigeria at the time, leading to frequent closures of Federal Universities and her parents took the decision to send her abroad to complete her studies in relative tranquility.

Being a UK citizen myself, I decided to follow her even though I had not been back to the UK since I left with my parents in 1976. I arrived in Manchester, in the north of England in the early 1990s, during a recession. I could not secure a professional job as an Engineer and as I did not like to be idle, I settled for a role as a security guard while I continued to look for better opportunities. I ended up working in this role for nine months.

During one of my moments of reflection, I remember thinking to myself, "I am not going to be a security guard forever; but while I am here, I might as well be the best security guard there is!" Fueled by this ambition to be the best there is, I applied, and was accepted for a store detective role with another security firm. I had gathered that one could earn more as a store detective and this inspired the switch.

It is good advice to fully understand the possibilities in your chosen profession.

The new firm offered me the opportunity to work in stores and as fate would have it, I soon had my first claim to fame. I was assigned as store protection to "Shadow" a famous bodybuilder from the world-famous Gladiators TV show, when they visited Manchester on a book promotion tour. Standing beside Shadow and his fellow bodybuilding colleagues was like a re-enactment of a scene out of the biblical story of David and Goliath. There I was, small in frame, like David, standing next to a huge Goliath of a man!

One of my other assignments at my new security firm was working at a care home for the elderly. One night, during a 16-hour shift, I spotted an advert for a graduate training position at the University of Manchester. I applied for the position and got the job. The role was a one-year placement however, at the end of the year, the University offered me a lifeline. I was asked to create a position that reflected the role I had been doing over the last year. So, I designed the role of the Technical Clerk, whose responsibilities revolved around energy efficiency and some accounting. Once the role was defined, it was advertised and twenty-four other people applied for the position. A rigorous interview process was set into motion and twenty-five of us were put through our paces. At the end of the process, I was offered the job which I continue to be grateful for.

Interestingly, the Technical Clerk role set me up for a potentially new career in either computer programming or accounting. I decided against accounting, because my dad is an accountant and I didn't want to compete with him in that space. I began teaching myself computer programming using Visual Basic. Within a short while, I had acquired sufficient knowledge and skill to apply for, and be accepted as a computer programmer at the College of Law.

After two years in that role, I got bored and wanted a new challenge. I applied for a computer programming role at GlaxoSmithkline (GSK), but unknown to me, my supervisor at the College of Law had also applied for the same role. It was an awkward moment spotting her seated in the lobby with me, waiting to be called for the interview. I am pleased to say that we remain friends till today despite the fact that I was eventually offered the role.

Reflecting on these events, I would like to point out a very important tip that really helped me with managing up for career progression:

The first thing you ought to do when you first join a new company is to find out the grading structure and the skills that you need to progress. On my second day at GSK, I said to my boss's boss, "I just looked at the pay scales and saw that you brought me in at the top of the scale for my grade. I just want to know when I can expect to get promoted".

He looked me in the eye and said, "Dude, people don't get promoted here until after five years!" Right there and then, I made up my mind that my case would be different. In the seven years that I was at GSK, I progressed from Senior Analyst Programmer to Lead Programmer, Business Analyst, Project Manager and finally, Programme Manager. Five roles in seven years! The peculiarities of each role taught me vital lessons on how to manage up, and some of the stories that I share in this book are a product of that phase of my working life.

While at GSK, I got to work on an outsourcing project, which involved using external consultant, and this got me thinking about the possibility of pursuing a career in Consulting. I applied and was accepted for a consulting role at Accenture which gave me the opportunity to work with some amazing companies within the UK and around the globe.

While working for Accenture, I was headhunted by PriceWaterhouseCoopers (PwC) for a managerial role. That was an offer I could not refuse, not just because the role was a promotion, but also because of the reputation of the firm. I joined PwC as a Manager, got promoted to Senior Manager and then became a Director. Unfortunately, I found myself in an unhealthy working relationship with my manager, and decided that it was time for me to jump ship.

I moved to Deliveroo, one of the fastest growing start-ups in the UK at the time, as Global People Operations Leader. It was while on this job that I got headhunted for my current role at Prosus, a technology investment company. I am currently a Global Vice President of People Technology at Prosus. At the time of writing this book, Prosus owns about thirty-one percent of Tencent. Prosus are big investors in Delivery Hero, Swiggy, Brainly, Code Academy and so on. We have a truly global reach.

So that, in a nutshell, has been my career journey to date. I have shared my journey so that you can have some context for the principles and ideas that I will now go on to share in this book.

Journaling Ideas

1. Reflect on your journey. Have you ever considered or highlighted the people who have helped you along the way?

2. Can you identify who your mentors were and how they have helped your career progression?

3. What inspiration(s) or lesson(s) can you draw from your background, past experiences or education that can help you appreciate where you are (or how far you have come) in your career right now?

_____

_____

_____

_____

_____

_____

_____

_____

_____

_____

_____

_____

_____

_____

2

4 Key Questions To Ask Before You Begin

WISDOM REQUIRES THAT before a man sets out to build a house, he counts the cost and ascertains what is required to build it. The same principle applies to the art of managing up for career progression. The following 4 questions need to be asked and satisfactorily answered before you begin the process of managing up for career progression.

1: Who are you?

If you don't really understand who you are, it is going to be extremely difficult for you to manage your career progression. What is your purpose? What is your intention? What drives you? You need to uncover the questions of purpose, intention, and drive in order to determine who you really are and as you discover yourself, you will be better suited to manage your career progression.

Furthermore, in the process of answering the question of who you are, you will discover what your strengths and weaknesses are. This is very important especially when you are in a place where you might feel stuck and don't know how to progress. Usually, this is due to not knowing or understanding your strengths and weaknesses.

As I write this, I vividly recall an experience I had at PwC, which pointedly illustrates the point I am trying to make. At that time, I was anticipating and getting prepared for a big promotion. Then, one day, out of the blue, my boss said to me, "I think you are ready for this (promotion), but you are missing something."

"What do you think I am missing?" I asked.

He responded matter-of-factly, "You surely deliver on the goods but you have a lot of spelling mistakes in your emails. Even when you write to clients, sometimes you still have these spelling mistakes. I think you need to get yourself checked out."

I appreciated his honest feedback, and took it in my stride. I agreed to undergo a dyslexia assessment, even though I was unsure what the outcome would be. My company generously paid for the assessment and at the appointed time, I went in to see the dyslexia specialist.

As the test progressed, the lady looked increasingly worried. After about an hour, she looked me in the eye and announced, "You are 100 percent dyslexic!" Before I could gather my thoughts, she continued, "I have no idea how you got to your position as director without having had any help before now."

Well, while I may not have had help up until that point, I knew I needed help going forward. So, with her guidance, we developed a strategy to help me manage the condition and deliver optimal results with fewer mistakes. I continue to use this strategy to date with remarkable results.

My point therefore is this: if you understand what your weaknesses are, you can address the problem. Take an audit of your life and identify your weaknesses. Do you lack the right kind of experience for a desired promotion? Or is it that your network is not strong enough for the higher managerial position that you seek? Do you lack the natural presence and charisma of a leader? Once you know your weaknesses, you can begin to focus on those things that need to be fixed or adjusted.

However, the audit of your life should not be limited to identifying your weaknesses alone. It should also extend to identifying your strengths and maximising them. One person's weaknesses are another person's strengths.

Once you know your strengths, you should also devote time to optimising them. A knowledge of your weaknesses and strengths are the foundations that will help you ensure you manage your job correctly.

2: Why are you managing up?

The second crucial question to ask yourself is why you are managing up? You need to fully find an answer to this question.

Understanding your why gives you clarity and enables you to be focused on your path. When you think through why you need to manage up, you are empowered to take on the challenges that will come your way.

Some people want to manage up so they can progress in the company. For others, it might be so they can help people avoid making the mistakes they made in their career journey. Some people give themselves to managing up because they lack confidence, or because they do not have a harmonious relationship with their managers. Some people manage up because they feel threatened at work or are worried about the future of the company they work with.

While the reasons for managing up will differ from one person to another, understanding your why is imperative before you take the big step.

3: What support do you need to be successful?

The third question you need to ask alludes to identifying the support structure you require to be successful. Many people fail to realise that success is built on the foundation of interdependence. This can also be the reason why people sometimes feel stale in their roles. They have not taken time to think through what support they need to be successful, let alone taking steps to seek and get such support.

In my case, I gave serious thought to the question of support. I was deliberate about getting the support I needed through mentoring and this has paid off greatly. In doing so, I found my way forward with managing up for career progression. Mentoring has been a key enabler in my career journey.

I have had different mentors at different stages of my career. I have sought out mentors who could help me succeed at specific phases of my career. Some mentorship relationships lasted longer than others depending on the peculiarities of the support I required. Sometimes I had a mentor for just a couple of months, to help me get over a hill, to help me maintain focus on the path ahead or to help me navigate out of a particularly precarious situation. I call this "FedEx Mentoring" – short-term mentoring with a particular objective in mind.

Understanding the support that you need is very important. Once you are clear about the support you need, and you seek out and get the support, the next bit of the journey becomes a little bit easier.

4: How can you improve your strengths and strengthen your weaknesses for career progression?

The fourth question to consider, when trying to understand who you really are and therefore what input you need from a mentor, is how best to maximise your strengths and minimise your weaknesses.

We all have things that we do well and things that we do not do so well but we put too much emphasis on our weak areas. Early on in my career I was told to go on training courses for mostly my areas of weakness. Then I attended The Global Leadership Summit in Chicago where I discovered this amazing book by Markus Buckingham and Donald Clifton - titled "Now, Discover Your Strengths".

My life changed completely after reading the book as it encourages you to give more attention to strengthening your strengths and managing your weaknesses.

I encourage you to take an inventory of your strengths and your weaknesses, then make a plan to strengthen your strengths and manage your weaknesses. A few times in my career journey, I have taken an area of weakness and turned it into an area of strength by dogged discipline and hard work.

When I started out in programming, I was definitely one of the weakest programmers in my team, but with hard work and discipline, I was able to turn my programming skills into a strength. I realised that if I stopped investing time and energy on strengthening a weakness, it became a weakness again.

As I sought to strengthen my weak programming skills, I discovered that I had a strength in user-centric design. Leveraging this strength actually improved my programming skills better as I was able to use graphical user interface to close my gaps. Today, I do not need to manage my programming weakness anymore as I have navigated my career down a different path.

Here is the win: managing my weakness and acknowledging it, helped me discover my strength – customer-centric design – and I still use the principles from that customer-centric approach in my work today.

Journaling Ideas

1. Answer these questions:
- Who are you?
- Why are you managing up?
- What support do you need to be successful?
- What are your strengths and weaknesses?

2. Who can you identify to assist you with answering these questions? (Example, a coach or mentor)

3. What weaknesses have you identified that could potentially be strengths if worked on?

3

3 Key Questions To Consider When Managing Up

NOW THAT YOU HAVE BEGUN the journey of managing up, there are vital principles you need to guide you along the way, lest you enter a ditch. Here are 3 (three) questions you need to answer as you progress in your journey in the art of managing up:

1: What Outcome Do You Want?

It is important you keep in mind what outcome you want at every juncture of your journey of managing up. In order to really optimise the art of managing up for career progression, understanding the outcome you want is very key.

To be clear, you may have to review and revise the outcome you want from time to time, since your experiences along the journey may open your eyes to new opportunities you never knew existed. Second, you may not always realise the outcome you want at every phase of the journey; nonetheless, expecting a definite outcome will keep you focused and disciplined.

2: What Environment Are You In?

The next question you need to ask yourself is what environment are you in? This question is crucial regardless of the challenges you may be facing or what your aspirations may be.

Is your business doing well or just getting by? Are you due for a promotion or are you seeking one in a year that the business is not doing well? One very vital question to ask as you seek to find a solution to these challenges is to understand the environment around the promotion process that you are going through. Career progression does not always mean a promotion. A lateral move sometimes can be the key to your career progression. The context you find yourself in is very key.

3: What's the Time?

This third question centres on timing. While on your journey of managing up, you need to ask if it is the time to seek promotion, time to move, time to take on more responsibility or time to relocate. Ask yourself: "what time is it?"

One thing you need to realise is that stepping up comes with a higher responsibility. The demands of the job you seek will likely be more intense than where you currently are. Are you prepared for that?

Don't seek change if you are not prepared to put in the extra hard work. There is almost certainly going to be more work to do. Preparation for change however transcends mental preparation. You ought to be mentally, psychologically, spiritually and socially prepared for any career progression. You ought also to evaluate what effect the new task would have on your family. Is your family prepared for the change that is bound to happen?

In summary, ask yourself: "Am I in the right season in my personal and family life for this change?" before taking the plunge.

These are the three questions you need to think about and settle in your mind in the course of managing up for career progression.

THE OUTCOME YOU WANT

THE ENVIRONMENT YOU ARE IN

THE TIME AND SEASON YOU ARE IN

4

Managing Up In A Healthy Environment

L ET US PROCEED to examine what it takes to manage up in a healthy environment. By a "healthy environment" I mean an office environment where there is congeniality and harmony among colleagues, and between supervisors/ managers and their subordinates. In essence, a working relationship that is bereft of bad emotions and negative undercurrents.

It is important to pay attention to this in order to preserve the positive energy within the environment, so that you would not be the reason why a rather healthy environment becomes frail and unhealthy. It is vital that we also think about the impact of a hybrid working environment and how we maintain healthy virtual work environments.

In my experience, there are 6 principles that can greatly help you manage up in a healthy environment. These are:

- Respect at All Cost
- Defer/Deflect - Never hog the limelight
- Understand the big picture
- Seek to understand
- Score big when your boss needs you to
- Understand the power of covering

Keys to Managing Up In A Healthy Environment

RESPECT AT ALL COSTS

DEFER AND DEFLECT: NEVER HOG THE LIMELIGHT

UNDERSTAND THE BIG PICTURE

SEEK TO UNDERSTAND

SCORE BIG WHEN YOUR BOSS NEEDS YOU TO

UNDERSTAND THE POWER OF COVERING

Respect at All Costs

The first principle for managing up in a healthy environment is to respect at all costs. Take note of the phrase "at all costs." This is an unusual type of respect. Indeed, if you really want to master the art of managing up, you need to cultivate the habit of respect, not only when it is convenient but even when it is not. You need also to be deliberate about inculcating this habit of unusual respect. Respect others at all costs. It is learnt, not inherited!

I call it unusual respect because it is not dependent on variables such as age. If you want to manage up in a healthy environment, do not only respect bosses that are older than you; respect them regardless of their age. In all but two jobs that I have had, my managers have been younger than me; yet, I respected them as though they were much older. Never let the age of your manager determine whether or not you will accord them the respect due to their position.

Another demand of this unusual respect is that you have to respect regardless of whether or not your manager likes you. It may be that your boss doesn't like you for some reason or for no reason at all. You still have a duty to respect them regardless. You may also not like your boss's style, personality or temperament; you still have a duty to respect them regardless.

To respect at all costs demands that you respect regardless of whether you are more knowledgeable than your manager in your discipline. You might be 100 percent more knowledgeable about the subject matter than your manager. What does it matter? You have a duty to respect your manager, not because he is more knowledgeable than you are but because he occupies a higher status than you do. It is a question of hierarchy. I can illustrate this with my experience. Throughout my career, I have found myself answerable to managers who are not as knowledgeable as I regarding the job I was doing. It never mattered, I still accorded them maximum respect because they were still my managers.

Finally, to respect at all costs demands that you respect your manager regardless of whether you are more experienced than them. At one stage in my career, in a managerial role, I had about 14 people reporting to me. These were heads of units–Head of Technology, Head of Administration, Head of Policy, Head of Global Mobility among others. Remarkably, none of them was over 28 years old (I was approaching my fifties at the time). These heads of units were leading teams with subordinates who were much older and experienced than them. Nevertheless, they were all leaders, and their team members accorded them the respect due to their positions and roles.

Sometimes, you may be more qualified or more experienced than your manager. You must accord them respect nonetheless. If you only respect your boss based on their experience or your perception of it, you will probably put a barrier on your career path.

To respect at all costs is both crucial and critical. It is key to managing up for career progression. Remember that your intention of managing up is to progress your career, and you cannot afford to allow any manager to be in your way. Therefore, keep your eye on the ball while you respect at all costs.

Our ability to respect at all cost has a way of creating an environment that leads to mutual respect. In a domain of mutual respect career progression discussions become easier and are more likely to result in the desired outcomes. The greatest partnerships are borne out of mutual respect.

Defer/Deflect - Never Hog the Limelight

Another principle of managing up in a healthy environment is to defer and deflect, and never to hog the limelight. This is yet another unusual but very important principle for managing up in a healthy environment. It is unusual because the popular view about how to take a quantum leap in career progression is that you must always be ready to showcase yourself. We have been taught to put ourselves out there, and literally draw attention to our work, saying "hey, look at what I did!"

What I have found out from experience is that the opposite is true. To manage up in a healthy environment, refrain from hogging the limelight. There is an intriguing experience on this subject while working as a manager at PwC, that I will love to share. I had just closed a massive deal worth over a million pounds in revenue. The interesting thing about the deal was that not only did I make a lot of money for the company, nobody was closing that kind of deal in my division at the time. You know what I did? I sent out a ton of emails to a group of partners and directors, saying "Hey, you know what, people? Look at what I did! Look at what I did! I mean, I closed this deal. You all tried to close the deal, but you couldn't. I did!"

My boss at the time, God bless his heart, tapped me on the shoulder, and said, "Stop trying to hog the limelight. You may have closed the deal but somebody brought you to the table. Someone availed you the opportunity to even try. You are certainly riding a good wave here. You can't afford to start hogging the limelight."

With the benefit of hindsight, those were wise words of caution did me a world of good. It was a much-needed call to apply the brakes and acknowledge the power of teams.

Interestingly, I soon found myself in a similar situation. I was in the middle of another assignment at the time and was suddenly asked to leave that role and join the negotiations with prospective new client–a bank that had reached a deadlock, with no headway in view.

As fate would have it, the boss who had given me that invaluable advice months ago, was the Lead Partner of this new team. that invaluable advice was the Lead Partner of the team that sealed the deal. I recalled his earlier advice and I kept quiet about my role in sealing the deal. I refrained from hogging the limelight.

Whenever people asked me how we did it, I deflected the limelight to my boss as the team lead. I refused to hog the limelight. Did it pay off eventually? Yes, it did!

The Partner was very generous with his commendations and endorsement of my abilities, which eventually led to my promotion.

The idea here is that you should work in partnership with your boss, and allow your boss to blow your trumpet; rather than you trying to blow yours and undermining your boss.

Remember, I said this should apply in a healthy relationship, where your boss is not trying to steal your work. In a healthy environment, it is easy for your manager to position you for promotion with their accolades. I got promoted through that experience because of my manager's recommendation.

Understand the Big Picture

Managing up in a healthy environment requires that you understand the big picture. This is very important. Sometimes when we engage in conversations around the subject of promotion or career progression, we overlook or close our eyes to the big picture. We may become so disoriented by our present challenges that we fail to step back and evaluate the events of the past in the light of the present situation. These are some of the questions to ask in order to understand the big picture by looking at past events:

1. What has happened so far on this journey?
2. What happened before you got there?
3. What happened to your boss before you got there?
4. What is the history of your firm and what is your own history?

A while ago, my boss's boss once said to me, "You know, it's going to take five years before you get a promotion." That statement was made on the backdrop of the ideal situation.

So, I researched past events and asked questions. By virtue of the stories I heard, I discovered that people who had spent five years did not in fact get promoted. I dug deeper and learnt that they did not get promoted because they were not willing to try new technology. They were comfortable with the status quo and were happy to do the same role for same job for several years without progressing. I knew I needed to do something different. I needed to try new technology. When I did so, I got promoted. That was how I was able to progress my career at GSK. I was promoted five times in the seven years I spent at the company.

Aside from understanding past events, you also need to understand current events so as to comprehend the big picture in your quest to manage up. You need to ask questions such as: "where is the company going? What is the company trying to do?" before pushing for promotion.

It could be that your company is trying to cut costs. If you push for promotion at such a time, there is bound to be a disconnect. It could be that your manager is managing a whole heap of different company dynamics; if you do not recognise this, you may feel isolated and mis-aligned from your manager thereby creating the wrong dynamics.

Having looked at past and present events, be sure to also look at future events. For instance, do you love the company you work for? Do you see a future for yourself in that company? If you work for a company you do not love, I suggest you begin to look at switching jobs to another company, because you cannot really progress in an organization that you do not like. If you do not like a company, it is very difficult for you to embrace the future of that company.

Finally, with regards to understanding the big picture, consider the location. By location, I mean the location of where your office is located within the company's structure. For example, if you work at the regional office, your ability to climb up the ladder would depend on how much of the high-grade decisions are made at the regional office as opposed to the headquarters. Sometimes, people have had to relocate from the regional office to the headquarters in order to get the promotion they desired. Some people think that this is science, but in reality, it is a combination of science and art. If there is no promotion available where you are, there is no point pushing for it while you are there. When it is clear that the pathway to promotion is not available in your current location you should look to relocate. If you do not make that change, you are likely to get frustrated about the unavailability of suitable roles for career progression. If you have hit the ceiling, you cannot possibly go any further. You really do need to understand the big picture in relation to your location. In a hybrid world, this particular point needs even more attention as remote working does not make the problem go away. Actually, in a remote working environment, one needs to be even more intentional about understanding the big picture.

I remember I once had a conversation with my career coach about this particular point, over dinner at a restaurant. I said to him, "I am looking at getting promoted." His response was unnerving, as he expressed the near impossibility of my aspiration at that time. He felt since it took him three years to get promoted to his current position, I was not ripe for promotion in his eyes. Yet in fairness to him, the reason why he took that position was because he did not understand the changing dynamics in the organisation. He did not realize that the company had moved on. They had created a new department. Growth was faster than it used to be. His understanding of where he thought the company was, was different from reality. He was missing the big picture.

Sometimes you need to take a step back from your normal way of thinking to understand the big picture and rightly position yourself for managing up. You need to reflect on past, current and future events, as well as your location. As you do this, you will gain significant insight that will come in handy when having conversations with your boss or your boss's boss and which could make all the difference regarding your aspirations.

Another thing that understanding the big picture helps with is building a network all the way up the ladder. This helps you understand the environment in which you are.

I recall an incident where my boss, who had been stuck in the same position for three years, asked me to ask his boss's boss whether he was in the right position to get promoted. In essence, my boss wanted me to inquire about his promotion based on my relationship with his boss's boss.

As you network and ask the right questions, you need to seek to understand not only the company's situation and your department's situation, but also your boss's situation. The reason for this is not far-fetched. If you fail to understand your boss's situation in the scheme of things, there will be a disconnect between you and your boss when you try to manage up for career progression. As you seek your boss's interest, your boss will also seek yours when you need them to.

Ask yourself: "Why?" Why does your boss want what they want? Why do they do what they do? Why do they have the objective that they have? In the next section, I will dive more into this when we look at the next element.

Seek to Understand

The fourth principle that can help you manage up in a healthy environment is to seek to understand, especially your boss's context. If your boss is in a situation where they are definitely looking to progress their careers, put your energies into helping them achieve their ambition because their progression is your progression. That synergy would make it happen fast and would also get you up faster than you thought.

A lot of people would have the attitude, "Well, if they want to progress, that's their business." That kind of thinking would not help you both. However, if you see it as your business, and as something that you need to put some energy into, guess what? Their progress will become your progress. I have seen this work out several times in my career.

Seek to Understand Your Boss's Why

Getting to know your boss is a key step in your journey of career progression. Your boss has a reason for why they do what they do. Getting to understand their why is key. Why did they take this particular job? Why do they do the things they do? Why do they manage the way they do? The more you understand their why the more you can align and once aligned the more you can achieve together.

I once had an experience that really underscored the importance of having such a conversation with your boss. I had a boss who was happy with his position and status. He was not thinking of getting a promotion anytime soon. Now, the way the organization was set up, he could remain in his position as long as he wanted, and if he was happy and not ready to move, there was not going to be a vacancy any time soon. The implication was that if I was going to realise my aspiration of career progression, I needed to switch jobs, as my boss's "why" did not align with my ambition.

Seek to Understand Your Boss's Intention

Once you understand the why of your boss's "why", the next thing is to understand their intentions, their goals and their plans. The more you understand, the more you get to know them. This requires building a solid relationship with your boss and this takes time and trust.

You need to get to a place where you are able to strike up a conversation with your boss over coffee, schedule a zoom meeting with them, or have a casual chit-chat with him over the phone, where you can say, "I am thinking of getting a promotion next year. What are your thoughts about that". As you know their intentions this will be an easier conversation, because it will be based on relationships.

Some bosses put up barriers, but in general, people want to connect. In understanding their why, you would know if they have been let down in the past by other employees for example.

Trust is a powerful currency that is required at the workplace, but more importantly, it is essential in a 1-1 relationship between a boss and an employee. With your boss's "why" understood, and trust established, you can then seek to understand your boss's intention, goals and plans.

When I was working in the payroll team at GSK, my client-boss at the time, the payroll manager, had one clear intention; in her nine years as payroll manager, she had never missed a payroll date or had payroll delayed. Her intentions were clear, 'Now that you work for me, please do not be the reason why we will miss payroll'. Once I understood her intention was never to miss a payroll, I was able to structure my work to meet that intention. When the time came for my promotion, she was super supportive because I had helped her deliver on her intention throughout the nine months I worked with her.

Think of this like a marketing strategy. If you intend to sell a product to someone, you need to understand their needs and ensure your product aligns to their needs. In the same way you need to understand your boss's needs before highlighting yours to them. Understanding your boss's family values or structure for instance, could help you understand why your boss functions the way they do. It may also help unravel their intentions.

Seek to Understand your Boss's Context

The reality of the workplace is that we work with humans. The time may come when we might be working with robots and artificial intelligent bots but for now we are working in a people centric workplace.

The complexity of human beings does manifest in the workplace and therefore impacts the managing up experience. As part of seeking to understand our boss, understanding their context is very key. Context includes factors such as the culture we are born into, the communities around us, the demands placed on us by society, on account of our gender or religious beliefs and so on. Take time to understand your boss's context. For instance, whether they are an only child, a twin or adopted all play into your boss's context.

If I look at my context, I was born to Nigerian parents in the UK, started my initial basic education in the UK, then finished primary, secondary and university education in Nigeria. I have travelled the world with my job and have been part of impact projects in remote parts of the world, bringing economic and social relief. All this makes up my context. If I am judged purely on the basis of the colour of my skin, my accent and job title, people will really miss my context. It is important to seek to understand. As a leader myself, I always want to understand the people I am leading. It definitely helps to know their context and understand the experiences that have shaped them.

Aside from understanding your boss's context, understanding your boss's fears is also important. Find out if your boss is secure in their role. Inquire if they are afraid of the circumstances they have found themselves in or if they are happy taking a leap into an uncertain future.

Going back to my boss who had been stuck in the same role for three years without a promotion, he got me to ask the Vice President of the company if he was in line for promotion. I was then in the awkward situation where I had to relay the Vice President's response which was "You need to deliver on what you were tasked to do last year. Only then will you be considered for promotion".

Things got even more awkward when I realised from the conversation that ensued afterwards that my boss was not at all willing to deliver on what he had been asked to do. More significantly, I realised I was not going to get promoted under this guy because he was not willing to do what was necessary for his own progression. Since a vertical move was not going to happen quick enough for me, I opted for a lateral move. Four years later, my boss and I became peers.

Seek to understand how you can stand out by your talent and skills

When I was pivoting from my security role to work at the University, I thought to myself, "There are going to be hundreds of applications, what can I do to make my application stand out?" In the "any other information" section of my application form, I decided to write: "I will give you one hundred and one percent (101%) commitment". I don't even know where that came from.

On reading my application form, the Deputy Director, John W, decided to interview me himself. He came into the interview room, looked at me and said, "I saw your one hundred and one percent commitment comment. What did you mean by that?"

I said, "I will go over and above to deliver for the University".

His response was "Interesting! I see that for the last 18 months you have been in security. So, I'm going to change your interview around. Whether or not you get this job will now depend on your ability to convince me that you can secure this university. If you've been doing security for the last 18 months, you should have learnt something from it, right? So tell me what you learnt. I took a deep breath and gave him a few suggestions on how security could be improved. At the end of the interview, as I walked out of the room, he said to me, "You have the job and on Monday, I am going to implement two things you said today!

John never directly managed me, but because I have a Civil Engineering background, he took a keen interest in me and was supportive. Two and a half years later, at my leaving party, with over 60 people present, he brought out my application form and said: "Sola wrote on his application form that he would give one hundred and one percent commitment. Do you think he delivered on that?" Everyone in the room chorused "Yes!".

In a nutshell, what I am saying is, put your skills to work. You know what you are good at. You are intelligent. You know what you can really bring to the party. If you put that to work, you'll be able to score big when your boss needs you to.

A lot of people go into career conversations and belittle themselves. Read, study, grow, make yourself better, because if you believe in progressing, sooner or later, doors will begin open for you to do just that. The question is, do you have the skill-set to manage your progression?

You need to understand the role that hard work and commitment play in getting ahead or breaking through to your desired role. Are you working at one hundred percent? Most people would probably say, "Yes! Infact, I am overworked!" but it is said that working at one hundred and five percent is just the right amount of stress that lends you to do your best work.

Furthermore, you need to seek to understand the place of team alignment. To use a football analogy, it is tempting to want to be a solo striker, to score all the goals by yourself rather than playing for and with the team of 11. However, if you are to manage up in a healthy environment, you ought to always think about the team that you are in. Your team mates are also trying to manage their jobs. You need alignment within the team and for everyone to be pulling in the same direction.

Don't focus on managing your career only, but focus also on managing what's around you. That's what's going to help you score big. If you can get aligned with the team, you collectively will score big for your manager. This leads me to the next point.

Score Big When Your Boss Needs You To

Scoring big for your manager is the number one thing that gives you career progression in a healthy environment. Please, always remember the caveat–this only applies to where you are working in a healthy environment and they believe in your expertise.

Go all out to score big for your boss when they need you to. Use innovation and creativity. When you bring those things together, you solve problems for your boss and that makes your boss look good. It gives him or her ammunition with which to put you forward for progression.

I was once in a situation where I had just been promoted to a new role. This was my first step into Human Resources Technology. I was nine months into the role and I was being innovative and creative in how I solved problems. I didn't know that my boss was keeping an eye on me. One day he called me into a room and said, "I've been watching you. I just want to let you know that I am leaving the company and I want you to take on this secret project that I have been working on. Only my boss in the US knows about it. I will be recommending you for the role".

I was intrigued. I asked him why he was putting me forward when there was a more senior person on the team who had acquired better knowledge and experience than I had. His reply was, "I am putting you forward because you have been innovative and you solved things we've been trying to solve for the last two to three years. You use innovative and creative ways to solve problems. The project I am working on is the outsourcing of our entire HR technology to America and the project will need that kind of skill set". All of a sudden, literally overnight, I was given a double promotion. Rather than report to a Director, I began reporting to a Vice President. I started working out of Philadelphia and North Carolina, traveling in and out of the US from the UK every two weeks. I began managing teams out of Manilla, Philadelphia and North Carolina. This was only possible because I scored big in the U.K payroll team, and this opened the door for me to work as a technology expert on a global transformation project. I learnt a lot of what I know today from that experience. To say it paid off would be stating the obvious. You also can get major breakthroughs such as this if you stick to this principle. Score big when your boss needs you to, because when it's time to return the favour, they will.

Understand the Power of Covering

The final principle regarding managing up in a healthy environment is to understand the power of covering.

Everyone has a covering. Even if you are the CEO of your company, you still have the covering of your Board. Your Board gives you air cover. They have a bird's eye view of the battles you are in right now.

When my boss covers me, I don't worry about politics. I just worry about getting the job done. That's what you need. You need to have that kind of an understanding. You need to get to a place where you are confident that your back is covered and you can stay focused on the things that need to get done. You need someone to fight the battles for you or with you. If you get drawn into political battles, you lose focus. That's why you need the covering because your covering gives you a defence.

I learnt this a while ago while working on a HR outsourcing project in Accenture. Even though I knew what needed to be done, the politics was too chaotic for me. This is often the case in the field of consulting. I was told I had to deliver a piece of work in four weeks. The client I was working with felt threatened by my work as it could mean she would eventually be out of a job. So, to her, I was enemy number one.

I had to recourse to the power of covering in order to complete the project in the required timeframe. My boss understood the political dynamics and he took the heat on my behalf. He explained the big picture to the managers and managed the politics while I focused on delivering the work. That strategy worked like magic. Whenever I had a relationship with my boss that gave me the air cover, it always allowed me to deliver my best work.

Whenever you feel overwhelmed, and your boss provides a covering, the tension is considerably eased. If your boss is not currently providing a cover for you in a challenging situation, then approach him/her for help with managing the issues. If you do not take any other thing away from this chapter, take this: If you can leverage your relationship with your boss correctly, they can give you a covering which will enable you to go into the trenches without any unnecessary distractions and do what you do best.

More importantly, having air cover makes discussions about a possible promotion much easier to have. I recall once being brought into the room of the Vice President of a company because my boss was worried that I was about to get a double promotion. The Vice President said, "Look, dude, I mean, we know what Sola does in this organisation. There is no conversation about this, just let the promotion go through!" That's the power of having the right covering. Often, you have to seek that out. It does not happen automatically.

Journaling Ideas

1. Of the six principles that I shared in this chapter, which one of them resonates the most with you?
2. Which ones do you need to work on to improve your chances of career progression?
3. Do you understand what your boss wants? Why did your boss take their current role? Are they looking to get promoted as well? Are they ambitious or are they satisfied with their current role? Why do they have the objectives that they have?
4. What opportunities to progress have you identified in your current role?

5

Managing Up in an Unhealthy Environment

I N THIS CHAPTER, we will examine the principles for managing up in an unhealthy environment.

Keys to Managing Up In An Unhealthy Environment

LEARN THE ART OF
LAYING LOW

SEEK OUT MENTORS
AND COACHES

STUDY TO SHOW
YOURSELF APPROVED

PROTECT OTHERS

RIDE THE WAVE

LEARN WHEN IT IS TIME
TO BOW OUT

As previously stated, an unhealthy environment is one that is toxic, especially between a manager and their subordinates. The focus of this chapter is therefore on how to manage your career progression in such an environment.

Here are 6 principles you need to do to achieve that goal:
- Learning the art of lying low
- Seek out Coaches and Mentors
- Study to show yourself approved
- Protect Others
- Ride the Wave
- Learn when it's time to bow out

Learning the Art of Lying Low

The first thing you need to do is to learn the art of lying low. This is very similar to the principle of refusing to hog the limelight; but it is in fact even deeper than that. Lying low is like when you are in a 30 mile per hour zone, you do not rev up. What you do to avoid getting a ticket is keep the car steady but below the limit. That's all you've got to do!

Get on with the job and do it right. Keep at it. Keep nailing it but never put your head above the parapet too much, since you are in an unhealthy relationship.

Let me explain what I mean with this example. I once worked with a boss who had very few Twitter followers. At the time, my company was driving Twitter as a way to promote our business and get more visibility in the digital ecosystem and they started tracking the best tweeters in the company. I had been tweeting regularly—almost once a week—and I gained a lot of followers. The company would publish a weekly poll and my name always popped up in the top three positions. That did not sit well with my boss, with whom I was in an unhealthy relationship at the time.

He summoned me and said, "Look, you need to focus on your work, and stop all this tweeting and social media thing. That is nothing but a distraction to you. I don't even know why you're doing that. You're behind on your projects but still have time for social media." Of course, it was not true that I was behind on my projects but that was his way of stopping me. It was pointless arguing with him or trying to explain my reasons for tweeting so regularly and, so I adopted the best approach to deal with the situation: I lay low.

Guess what happened next? He started tweeting endlessly, and in time, he rose to become the top tweeter. If I had any doubt that I needed to get out of that unhealthy environment, that episode eradicated all doubts. It became abundantly clear that every time I delivered something, every time there was a celebration, every time a client appreciated my work, every time I made a sale, he got more and more worked up and provoked.

My mentor at the time had been warning me that there was no alternative but to get out of the system. It was either I left, or I stayed and died professionally on that job. After the tweeter incident, I got back to my mentor and we planned my exit.

Learning the art of lying low really helps you remove the unhealthy tension that you may be faced with. Also in most unhealthy relationships, there are underlying issues which you might stir up even further if you do not lie low. In an unhealthy relationship you want to ensure that you are not in an abusive situation. If there is verbal or mental abuse please reach out to your HR teams. I had to do that also at one point just to make sure I was not going through the process alone.

This leads me to the next principle that would help you manage up in a healthy relationship.

Seek out Coaches and Mentors

When you are in an unhealthy environment you really need to seek out mentors and coaches. You can't survive without them, so seek them out. While mentors and coaches are also needed in a healthy environment, they are even more urgently needed in an unhealthy environment, as they are critical to your survival.

Some of the few mentoring relationships I have had started when my mentee was in an unhealthy situation and sought my counsel on how to navigate it. We always need people who can help us make sense of the madness around us. That essentially was what I needed during the Twitter experience at work. I sat down with my mentor and we talked about it and we were able to see the facts and underlying issues.

To bring further clarity, my mentor agreed to have a conversation with my boss. An hour and a half later, he said,

"You need to leave this guy, because you will not progress with a boss like this. There's no way you're going to be able to progress with this guy's mindset." So, I left the company. I am glad that I did because I would not be where I am today if I had not made that move. The importance of coaches and mentors to your career progression cannot be over-emphasised.

Mentors have this ability to see greatness in you and draw it out. A mentor takes you on the road they have been on and shows you shortcuts to get to the destination. My mentor was amazing at helping me navigate to where I am today. Helping me carefully and wisely navigate out of an unhealthy environment and finding an environment where I could thrive and grow.

66

A mentor takes you on the road they have been and shows you shortcuts to the destination.

Study to Show Yourself Approved

One of the keys that can help you manage your career in an unhealthy environment is to keep improving yourself. Study to show yourself approved, not only by your manager but by all who are observing you. Whether your manager likes you or not, you need to keep being approved and to be the best version of you. One way of doing that is to keep yourself updated with trends and changes in the marketplace.

There is always a need to prove your mettle in an unhealthy environment. There is hardly a better way of doing so than to study to show yourself approved.

Besides, if you fail to do so, you will most likely find yourself running into roadblocks such as unending criticisms of your work and person. People will come at you and say things like, "You didn't deliver on X or Y"; "You were sloppy at this" or "You were unproductive at that."

Always be ahead of the game. Always know what you need to do, and do it. If you adhere to this, you can actually turn an unhealthy environment into a healthy one. It does not always happen, but it can.

I recall an experience where I had the fortune of turning an unhealthy relationship to a healthy relationship. At the time, I was at the bottom of the class. I was the worst programmer. Recall that I stumbled on programming accidentally. It was not a career I set out to pursue from the onset. I had taught myself the little I knew. When I found myself in a job in the

College of Law where it was evident to all that I was the least performer, I knew I had to do something radical about the situation.

What did I do? I studied. I studied and studied again. I worked hard until I was named the best programmer in the department. My boss at the time, with whom I was in an unhealthy relationship, could not help but notice the transformation. Once he noticed that I was improving myself, an unhealthy relationship turned to a healthy one. Interestingly, we are good friends now, even till today.

Protect Others

In an unhealthy environment, you might not be the only one feeling the heat of toxicity. So you need to be on the lookout for others and protect them. This was certainly the case in the Twitter incident I relayed earlier. I realised I wasn't the only one getting that kind of treatment from my boss. Others were also experiencing difficulties with him. So, without resorting to backbiting, I began to work with my colleagues to navigate through the overbearing situation. I went to some and affirmed that they were not alone, while admonishing them to keep their eyes on the prize and study to show themselves approved. That helped, I saw renewed vigour and vitality. I saw determination to keep their eyes on the prize of career progression. And for some, they had to navigate to a place where there was better clarity of purpose.

Ultimately, something good will come out of protecting others. It is a time for you to grow in leading others. Leadership is key to managing up in an unhealthy environment. Leading people in an unhealthy environment with your words and actions will be greatly appreciated by the people around you. No one likes a toxic environment and if you can somehow diffuse the tension, it will truly protect and help people.

Ride the Waves

The fifth principle for managing up for career progression in an unhealthy environment is to "ride the wave." This is different from the principle of studying to show yourself approved which I discussed earlier.

To ride the waves, you must first have studied to show yourself approved. You must have studied to show yourself as a good surfer before you can ride the waves. You must have carefully prepared yourself for what it takes before you go out on the water. Even though you do not determine and cannot predict the waves and turbulence that will come at you, you can be well prepared for any eventuality.

In relation to managing up in an unhealthy environment therefore, you have to be well prepared. Be prepared to make the change if that is what is needed. Be ready to do your work the right way if that is what is required. Be prepared for whatever comes your way.

In an unhealthy environment, it is very likely that you will be tossed by the waves back and forth, in ways you least expect. When you make moves to get promoted, it is likely that you will be made to seem unfit and not ready for promotion. Be prepared to ride the waves.

Without a doubt, one of the most dramatic incidents in my career path was one that occurred when I had just gotten promoted. My boss and I had a very toxic, unhealthy relationship. It was so bad that I could not point to any particular reason for the hostility. Maybe it was my colour, or perhaps it was envy as a result of my promotion. Maybe it was my guts or energetic spirit. It could have been anything. All I knew was that he was throwing waves my way from every angle. It got so bad that he pointedly asked me: "Are you okay with this level of disruption that your boss is throwing at you?" I was mortified.

One day, he called me into a room and said, "I am going to mark you down as an underperformer and I am going to put you on a development plan." To put some context to that statement, you need to understand that I was top of my promotion class. In fact, my promotion was based on the fact that I scored the highest points in the entire division for the year. There was nothing in my track record to suggest that I was an underperformer. I was mortified.

I cascaded his decision to the HR, and they took it up with him. HR said to him, "It is not possible for anyone to drop from being one of the highest performers to being an underperformer in less than 6 months." He was reminded that 6 months prior, I had been top of the class. Such a drop in performance is ridiculously unaligned. HR intervened and I was given a lifeline and enough time to gather my thoughts, come out of the shock and ride on the waves ahead of me. HR is a powerful resource for you in any organisation particularly when you find yourself in an unhealthy environment.

I am so grateful to all the help that the HR function or the modern day People function have given me personally over the course of my career. They are truly there to help, so do reach out to them.

When the initial move to mark me as an underperformer did not work, HR informed my manager that he was duty bound to find me a mentor, and to give me a specific piece of work that could be tracked. It was suggested that I should be given my own product to own. My manager then decided to throw me the most turbulent wave ever. He assigned me a product to lead that had done no business for four years. The company had made no sales on this product for years. The unsuccessful department had previously been led by a senior and more experienced colleague.

Now if the senior and more experienced colleague had limited success, what hope did I have? The assignment was basically a ghost town, a poisoned chalice. Nonetheless, I said to myself, "I am going to ride these waves. I am not going to allow this unhealthy relationship to truncate my career progression." So, I rode on the waves.

About a year later, by the next performance round, I had developed a 10-million-pound pipeline and signed two million pounds worth of business in what had hitherto been a dead area. This is what I mean when I say you've got to ride the waves. It is quite different from starting to show yourself approved. Riding the waves means developing a thick skin and driving against the torrents with determination and tenacity. It is riding the waves even while anticipating even more turbulence ahead. When the storm comes at you to drown you, you rise above it. You do not become complacent. You may have gone past waves that are only two centimetres. Do not become complacent. Keep an eye out for the next big wave that is coming from thousands of miles away. You always have to be ready to ride on the waves.

The most powerful thing I learnt in this season is that people are watching how you respond to what is thrown at you. Years later after this experience a few people reached out to tell me how impacted they were by how I just kept a good attitude and focused on delivery. So there was an unexpected byproduct of that experience—not only had I proven myself, I had shown others how to respond to similar situations by my actions and attitude.

Learn When It Is Time to Bow Out

The final thing to do in an unhealthy relationship, and I've had to do it a couple of times, is to learn when it is time to bow out.

Recall the story about my manager who disagreed with my desire to be promoted? How did that end? Well, at the time, I just looked at him and said, "This is the last conversation we are going to have about this. You will no longer be my manager, and this dinner is over!" He was more nervous than shocked about what I said because he knew that if I had gone to his boss to protest that the relationship wasn't working out, his performance review would have been impacted negatively.
So he asked me for a favour. He said, "Do not tell my boss

that we are not working together anymore until after the performance review."

"Okay, I can do that. I can give you that." I responded.

Eventually I changed positions and I switched to working for a different manager. Within six months of that change, I got promoted to the same level as my former manager. Four years later, I was promoted to Director and ended up being his supervisor and manager on a few projects. I was gracious to him and we worked well together.

It is key to learn when to bow out. Bowing out of the relationship with my manager gave me an opportunity to grow and develop. I was working in consulting at the time and it is easier to change your people manager in Consulting as they are typically not your assignment manager. Changing managers is probably not as easy if you are being managed by your department boss or if the headcount and department structure is limited.

There have been times in other places where I have had to bow out by completely leaving the organisation.

Conclusion

THANK YOU FOR COMING on this journey with me, as we have explored the concept of managing up for career progression. Looking over my personal life and career journey, I am so grateful for all the mentors that helped me along the way. I am grateful for the lessons I learnt which gave birth to this book. I am really hoping that this book has been a helpful resource to you.

We are all on a journey to a destination where dreams and visions are fulfilled. It does not matter where you are in your career journey, you have the power to influence your journey by applying the right principles.

I would definitely choose working in a healthy environment over an unhealthy one any day but I also acknowledge both experiences have taught me valuable lessons which have collectively made my career journey much more interesting.

I hope that you can find practical ways to implement the elements shared in this book and as a consequence, have a more fulfilling career journey.

I would like to give a shout out to all the managers and leaders out there. You have a tough job, and the environment your employees work in has a way of influencing their careers. I hope this book will help sharpen your own awareness of the environments we intentionally or unintentionally create. Here is hoping that people find joy and fulfilment in working for you, as you make room for their growth and career progression.

I know that some of the things that I have discussed in this book may require deeper exploration in a one-on-one coaching or mentoring relationship. I would encourage you to reach out to your mentor, your coach, your leadership teams, or a good friend and work through the questions in the book. This will help crystallise the concepts contained here.

After running my first webinar on this topic, I had the privilege of leading two masterclasses for 4 weeks, where we worked through the content with live examples. It was a thrilling exercise for the cohorts and I. Following that programme, everyone in the cohort either got promoted, found new jobs, or have improved their relationships with managers. And above all, they have all progressed in their careers.

My last word to you is this: you have what it takes to effectively manage up and get the career progression you desire and deserve. Press forward!

Questions and Answers

I N THIS SECTION, I share some questions that were raised during a webinar I ran on the art of managing up for career progression. I hope you find my answers helpful.

Q1: What are your thoughts on the best time to quit an unhealthy environment

A: I think there are some principles that we need to keep at heart. The first is: what event are you in right now? If you are in the middle of a life changing event, this may not be the right time to quit. For instance, if you or your wife have just had a baby, it may not be the right time to leave or change your job. It may be more prudent to manage the unhealthiness in the workplace until you get to a position where you can comfortably apply for jobs. When you get another job, then you can pull out. Largely, it depends on the environment you find yourself in.

However, this depends on whether you are in a healthy or unhealthy environment. If you are in an unhealthy environment and you cannot fix it, the best thing to do is to pull out when the time is right.

Q2: Women often don't seek the spotlight, which is a problem for their promotion prospects. They think hard work is enough and have to be encouraged to be visible. What would you advise?

A: It is true that women find themselves in this disadvantaged position where they are not encouraged to go for promotion. In this regard, I applaud PWC UK actually, because they recently published their gender gap and are working really hard to close that gap. The reason they are working hard at this is largely due to lady called Laura Hinton, who was one of my mentors. Laura is passionate about helping people, especially women, find meaningful progress in their career. Her work is enormous because when you are in a place where there are no women at the top, it becomes very hard to find a role model to show you how to get there. So, my advice to women is to get mentors, get coaches, and look beyond your immediate sphere. Look for people who can help you understand the environment that you are in.

Interestingly, women often work hard and smart right through school. They get better grades than boys and men but when it comes to the workplace, they do not raise their visibility or realise the need to actively seek the spotlight. That is why we have few women in leadership today. They have been culturally and socially taught to put their heads down and work hard, rather than to raise their heads up and be recognized.

I often coach women to actively seek the spotlight, to seek out projects that would raise their visibility within the organisation. Remember that spotlighting your work is very different from hogging the limelight. Don't mix them up.

When you talk about salaries with a group of women, they become very shy because they do not understand how it works.

What I try to do is to push women forward. I push them to look into the pay structures of their organisations and to think about how to get an increase. I teach them to ask for what they want with confidence. I ask the question: "How would you put a market price on what you're doing?" The reason for this question is because women tend not to think like that. They tend to think solely about doing the work and doing the right thing. Men are always thinking about pay and ensuring they get the right pay, whether in a job interview or at a performance review.

Some will say that I am genaralising but the truth is men are more confident than women when it comes to negotiating pay.

Think through it all. Assume that you are approaching the highest point of your current pay grade. How are you going progress? A lot of people do not give this serious thought. My advice is, look at the pay grade for the next level and think about the skills that are needed to progress to the next level.

Ask yourself these questions:
Where do I feature in this? Am I in the right position? Would I get extra money if I am given a promotion?

Q3: How do you strike the balance between not hogging the limelight and selling yourself?

A: That's always a difficult one. I learnt this lesson experientially, making many mistakes along the way.

You should not hog the limelight; but you should sell yourself–I mean you should make noise about it! There is a delicate balance between the two. A lot depends on the relationship that you have with your manager. A lot also depends on what you have had to grapple with mentally. A lot depends on the right timing. I have been in a place where I have had really inspirational coaches or mentors who talked me out of selling myself at the time. They said to me, "dude, this is not the time to sell yourself. Not today; not at this event."

I will tell you a story which, though has nothing to do with work, centres on the power of having people that can speak into your life.

While at University, I published a newsletter which got a wide circulation and readership. So, I thought to myself, "I'm going to do a sequel!"

I prepared the manuscript, printed copies, and took them to Chris, my spiritual mentor at the time. I said to him, "I have written a sequel to my successful newsletter. May I proceed with distributing it?" "No!", he said bluntly. "I want you to sit there and rip up every single copy of the newsletter because today is not the day for the limelight!" I was deflated. I had spent my hard earned money to produce this newsletter. The lesson I learnt at that moment was this: Do not write simply because you are riding on a popularity wave. Rather, write because you have a passion for the subject.

That incident happened almost thirty years ago but I am so grateful to Chris, for the life lessons he taught me, albeit in a rather painful manner at the time. He had the courage to mentor me that way.

Q4: When do you tell your boss you want progress?

A: This is similar to asking how long a piece of string is. I think you need to understand your boss's intention and understand your own path also.

To illustrate with my experience, recall that I arrived at the College of Law an underdeveloped programmer. I was the least capable programmer in the team, but I discovered I had a knack for Graphic User Interface design and I later became the lead developer on some of the projects. I was even forced to take on some projects, because of my skills and creativity.

Even before I started looking for a new job, I said to my manager, and said, "I can't see how I can progress here! I am going to leave!" Audacious right? Nevertheless, he agreed with me!

He agreed that I would eventually have to leave, but asked what could they do, in the meantime, to keep me engaged? While the times may be different, the principles still apply. However, I think a lot of it will depend on your temperament, your confidence, and your manager.

There are a lot of things that come into play here. However, the best thing to do is bounce the idea off a coach, a mentor or a friend. If you don't have one of those people to bounce the idea off, you won't have the privilege of an independent mind analysing the situation for you.

It's probably easier to speak with your manager about career options if you have a good working relationship with them than if you don't.

Q5: Have you worked for managers with different ethnicities? How has emotional intelligence played a part in managing a change?

Emotional intelligence is absolutely crucial. You could write a book about how to use emotional intelligence in management.

I have worked in teams with diverse ethnicities. I have worked in different countries. As a Consultant, I have been on projects with all kinds of people from all kinds of backgrounds.

Based on my own experience, I don't think ethnicity matters. What matters is understanding people as human beings. Understanding their wants, and desires, and perhaps overlay it with some understanding of cultural background. There is a great book on this topic called "The Cultural Map" by Erin Meyer that I highly recommend.

Q6: What advice do you have on finding a mentor before you make a great transition?

What does it mean to find a mentor? Look for people that inspire you. Look for people who encourage you or encourage others. Sometimes you find a mentor because they're mentoring other people. You find a mentor at a forum where you can connect with what the speaker is saying. Sometimes it just comes out of a relationship. But I would say the best way to find a mentor is to look for somebody who inspires you.

In addition, when looking for a mentor, you look beyond your organisation. Approach people on LinkedIn. There are many tools you can use to find a mentor, especially now that the world is more globalised. The opportunities are so much wider. You do not necessarily have to meet with a person physically before you can connect with them as it was in the past. We live in a hybrid world now. Leverage the opportunities presented by the age in which we now live.

Q7: What did you put in place as a dyslexic person to help you?

A: Unfortunately, by the time I was diagnosed, I was already a long way down my career journey. I remember the assessor looking at me and saying: "I don't know how you got here, so I don't want to mess with the formula. It looks like you've created a formula by yourself to manage your dyslexia." Somehow, I learnt to cope. With hindsight, I encourage parents to pay attention to how their kids learn and try and pick up on any learning difficulties early.

My assessor said: "Some of the tools I can recommend for you are to use a spell checker more and use speech/voice to text technology.

Speaking comes naturally to me, and it is how I compensated for my learning disability. I compensate by speaking. I can speak to anybody. I have no fear of speaking to a crowd.

My writing is where I need help. Yet I have written four books. What I do is to get an editor who can read, proofread it and make sure it is all good. Even the slides I use for presentations, I check with people as they will be able to see through the things I may have missed because of my disability. That is how I manage it.

A lot however depends on how early you begin to manage it. One of my kids also has dyslexia and luckily, we caught it at about the same time as mine. She has got a lot more coping mechanisms to help her in her classes. She is currently at University, studying her course of choice.

In summary, managing a learning disability like dyslexia, largely depends on where you are on your journey, how willing you are to confront it and how you would like to get help. So, I would say: get help as soon as you have identified your weakness, and it will make your journey easier.